Prayers
for
DIFFICULT
TIMES
for Kids

Print ISBN 978-1-68322-276-7

Published by Barbour Books, an imprint of Barbour Publishing, Inc., 1810 Barbour Drive, Uhrichsville, Ohio 44683, www.barbourbooks.com

Our mission is to inspire the world with the life-changing message of the Bible.

Member of the
Evangelical Christian
Publishers Association

Printed in the United States of America.
06057   0518   BP

Prayers
for
DIFFICULT
TIMES
for Kids

MATT KOCEICH

BARBOUR BOOKS
An Imprint of Barbour Publishing, Inc.

Contents

Introduction

"For I know the plans I have for you,"
declares the LORD, "plans to prosper
you and not to harm you, plans to
give you hope and a future."
JEREMIAH 29:11

● ●

You are so important. Your life matters, and God has special plans for you. The more time you spend talking and listening to Him, the more you will understand just how much He loves you.

But life is tricky. Some days are great. You find yourself having fun with your friends and nothing goes wrong. Everything feels right.

Then, in a blink of an eye, everything seems to fall apart. Friends seem distant, school becomes a challenge, and you feel like you don't fit in. But the good news is that even though things change, God does not. He is trustworthy! All the time!

Prayer is a special way you can stay connected with your heavenly Father. The Bible is full of people who talked to God during good and bad times. These devotions and prayer starters draw inspiration from those stories by helping you remember how God blesses His children. Use the prayer starters in each section to help get your quiet time going. Let them be the beginnings of great conversations between you and your Creator. He loves you so much and wants to use your life to accomplish great things.

BEING BULLIED

The LORD is good, a refuge in times of trouble.
He cares for those who trust in him.

NAHUM 1:7

. . . .

Being bullied isn't fun. When someone is ugly to you with their words or actions, your heart feels hurt and it's hard to think straight. You're tempted to get angry and defensive. It's easy to become scared and worried. Being bullied might even make you think that God has gone away and left you all alone.

But God reminds you in His Word that He forever guards you everywhere you go (Psalm 121:8) and that He will never leave you (Deuteronomy 31:6). God knows how you feel. His Son Jesus was bullied when the soldiers laughed and spit at Him. Jesus felt just like you do.

Talk to your parents and teachers about your situation. And don't forget Jesus is your shield. Remember, as a child of the King, you are dearly loved and protected. Keep your faith in Jesus because He will never let you down.

Lord Jesus, please watch over me. Wrap me in Your mighty arms. You conquered death, so You can definitely protect me from the ones who bully me. Thank You for going before me today. Thank You for caring about everything I'm feeling. You are my shield.

Even though I feel nervous about being bullied, I know that You are helping me not to worry. I praise You for guarding me. God, please fill my heart with peace that only comes from You. Help me rest in Your shadow and have confidence that Your powerful hands never stop holding me.

Today is a new day, Father. Your promises remind me to rejoice because You have spread Your protection over me. The Bible proclaims You are the Mighty One. Fill my heart with that truth. Teach me not to be afraid because You are always with me!

FEELING LIKE I HAVE TO BE PERFECT

He is the Rock, his works are perfect,
and all his ways are just. A faithful God
who does no wrong, upright and just is he.
DEUTERONOMY 32:4

. . . .

There are days when you look around and think that other people are perfect. It seems like everything they do works out, while everything you try messes up. You start to think if only you work harder, your life will look like theirs. Trying to be perfect and look good in front of other people starts to feel like a heavy weight in your hands. It's not easy, and it drains your energy.

God did not create you to carry this kind of heavy load or burden. You weren't made to try harder or become someone you weren't made to be. God made you special and wants you to see your life the way He sees it. You are His child. He is the perfect One.

So don't put pressure on yourself to be perfect. No matter what situation you're in or what kind of job you have been given, through God's love and presence you can do it all (Philippians 4:13).

Lord Jesus, please help me. I try so hard
to be perfect, and it's getting frustrating.
Help me remember that You alone are the
perfect One. Teach me not to worry and to
leave the outcome to You. Help me see each
day as a chance to rest in You instead
of trying to be perfect.

Father God, I see so many of my friends
trying to be perfect, and it makes me want
to be like them. I find myself wanting to fit
in and work extra hard to do everything
right. I spend a lot of my time hoping I don't
make mistakes. Please show me how
to let that go and trust You.

Help me remember, Jesus, that You alone are perfect. Help me remember that my life is wrapped in Your mighty arms. Help me remember that You love me for who You made me to be. Nothing more, nothing less.

TEASED BECAUSE OF MY FAITH

Be on your guard; stand firm in the faith;
be courageous; be strong.
1 CORINTHIANS 16:13

· ·

You matter. You are important, and the God of the universe thinks you're special. Don't forget this. The enemy tries to attack your hope in many ways. Being teased isn't fun, but remember those words aren't true. When other people say things to make you feel bad, don't forget who you really are: a chosen child of God!

If the day comes when you are teased, especially because of your faith, be strong. Remember, hurtful words are not a judgment of you, but simply the sad proof of sin. Remember that it's always helpful to confide in a trusted adult.

And, don't forget to hold on to the promise Jesus made when He said you'd be blessed when people make fun of you because of Him (Matthew 5:11–12). You mean the world to God, and He is so proud of you.

Lord, You are my shield. Teach me how to listen to You more. Teach me how to not worry when other people make fun of me because I love You. Help me dig deeper into Your Word and find peace in Your promises. Thank You for loving me.

I know You are holy and I know You made me. Help me focus on these truths instead of the hurtful words that come because of my faith. Lord, You are worth everything I have, so please continue lifting my head so I can see past the pain.

God, give me strength. Help me stand strong in my faith. Help me focus on You all day long. I know that You hold my life in Your hands, and that's the truth I will think about today. You keep Your promises, and I'm so thankful that You do.

STRESSED OUT

Cast your cares on the Lord and he will sustain you; he will never let the righteous be shaken.
PSALM 55:22

· ·

All through the Bible, God gives examples of His children in stressful situations. But, in each of those stories, God is always with them just as He is always with you. Even though the stress is like a weight that holds you down, God never leaves your side. Tell Him everything. Don't hold any of the things that cause you to stress in, because He wants to hear it all.

Also, telling your parents about your stress is a good way for you to know you're not alone. You can keep a prayer journal, too, to help get your feelings down on paper. It's a great way for you to see how God helps you over time.

As you go through your day, please remember that God is holding you through every situation. He made you and wants you to let Him be your source of peace. You are loved.

God, I don't know how to handle this stress.
Life is crazy right now. I can't make sense
of it all. A lot of my worries come from not
knowing what's going to happen tomorrow.
I get overwhelmed with thinking the hard
times are never going to end.

Lord, I don't like the way this stress feels.
It seems like the hard parts of life are too
much to handle sometimes. Please help me.
I know You are my Almighty God. I know
You are bigger and stronger than my stress.
Help me trust in You more today.

Father, I pray that my faith in You is strengthened. This stressful season isn't bigger than You! You are my God who cares about everything I'm feeling. Please fill my heart with Your unending love, and show me how to keep my eyes on You.

When I'm Anxious

Do not be anxious about anything, but in every situation, by prayer and petition, with thanksgiving, present your requests to God.
PHILIPPIANS 4:6

. . . .

Being anxious gives you an opportunity to lean in closer to God. Your heavenly Father is right there by your side. Trust Him. Tell Him everything that's weighing you down. Don't forget that God loves you more than anything.

The Old Testament prophet Jeremiah said that God is our "refuge in time of distress" (16:19). God did not make you to be worried and go through every hour troubled by anxiety. Just look to His Word! Jeremiah also said, "LORD, you understand; remember me and care for me" (15:15).

Your awesome Creator, your mighty Protector, wants you to live right in the center of His glorious hope. Psalm 42:5 says, "Put your hope in God." When you start to feel waves of anxiety crash over your heart, remember God's promise that Jesus is your peace (Ephesians 2:14). Give God your fears, and don't forget that He loves you!

Father God, please hear me. Hear me because I'm anxious and I don't know what to do. Help me lean in and grow close to You now. I feel weird because all I can think about is the stress. I know You're there. Please help me conquer these feelings.

God, You made me. Please keep guiding me down the path of Your will for my life. Please remind me how important I am to You. I know that Your Word reminds me to rest in the peace of Jesus, and that's exactly what I want to do. Show me how to let go of my anxious thoughts.

Lord, all I want to do is live a
life that brings You glory. You are
worth everything to me, and I
don't want to let my anxiety stand
in the way of Your love. Teach me
all about Your plans for my life.

Making Hard Choices

*If any of you lacks wisdom, you should ask
God, who gives generously to all without
finding fault, and it will be given to you.*
JAMES 1:5

. . . .

You are not alone. God is with you. He loves
you so much that He will never leave you. If
you're in a situation where the choices aren't
easy, go to God in prayer. The devil wants you
to believe that the easy choices are always the
right ones.

But God is using you to do great things. He's calling you to be courageous in your home and school. This means you will face hard choices that stretch your faith. It might be deciding not to laugh when a friend is making fun of someone, or not listening to a song that is inappropriate just because your friends like it.

Your worth and identity are in Jesus. Don't worry about what other people think. When you find yourself in a place where making the hard decision is right, know that God is on your side, and make it!

Lord, please give me wisdom and strength. Help me make the right choice every time I'm faced with a hard decision. Thank You for always being with me. Sometimes I'm tempted to take the easy way. Teach me to stay focused on all Your promises!

Jesus, help me remember all the hard choices You made. You left Your throne to save me. You took up Your cross so that all of my sins would be forgiven. You stood up for people who didn't have a voice, and You gave up Your life so I could live with You forever.

Help me see this new day as a gift.
Thank You for Your love, Lord.
Show me how to love You more,
and guide me down the right path.
Give me the courage to make
the hard choices in life!

My Siblings Drive Me Crazy

*I call on the LORD in my distress,
and he answers me.*

. . . .

Some days it's hard to deal with your siblings. In fact, sometimes the arguing and disagreements might go on for days, weeks, and even months at a time. But your siblings are not your enemies. The devil is your enemy, and he tries hard to make you believe that your worth is in the words and actions of your brothers and sisters. Don't forget that your worth is in Jesus, your mighty King. Your worth is in what He says and what He has done for you!

Stress caused by siblings is found in many Bible stories. Cain was jealous of his brother Abel (Genesis 4). Esau was jealous of Jacob (Genesis 25). And Joseph's brothers didn't like the way their father seemed to show favoritism to their brother, who was a dreamer (Genesis 37).

God made everyone in your family different. Use this knowledge to overcome your family struggles, and honor and respect your siblings.

Lord, my siblings do things that get on my nerves. Help me to slow down and think about my words. Help me to practice being kind to them and to show them the love You keep showing me. God, You know my heart. Teach me how to be more like Jesus every day to my siblings.

I feel sad sometimes because it seems like my siblings don't understand me. Help me to listen more. Help me hear what they say. I want to remember that they have feelings, too. Help me not to become selfish but become the person You made me to be. Help me serve my family.

Father, I pray that You will give me the courage to have a humble heart, to be able to apologize when I need to. Help me be the kind of sibling who asks for forgiveness and who forgives. Jesus, You love unconditionally, and I want to be just like You.

Someone Close to Me Died

For we believe that Jesus died and rose again,
and so we believe that God will bring with
Jesus those who have fallen asleep in him.
1 Thessalonians 4:14

. . . .

When someone you know passes away, it's very
hard to understand. Their life meant so much to
you, and their absence doesn't make sense. But
take hold of God's promises, and find comfort
in His never-ending love for you!

The Bible says that those who believe in Jesus will be with Him in heaven after they die. Jesus even said that He was going ahead to prepare a place in heaven for all of His people (John 14). Find hope in the fact that He is "the resurrection and the life." Jesus said in John 11:25, "The one who believes in me will live, even though they die." And Psalm 116:15 says, "Precious in the sight of the Lord is the death of his faithful servants."

God wants you to share your heart with your parents and family. Let them know how you feel, and ask them questions. You are not going through this hard time alone!

Lord, it hurts when I think about this.
My loved one is gone. Please help me
remember that I will see them again in
heaven. Show me the truth in all of Your
promises. Help me find rest in the shadow of
Your arms. Hold me through this tough time.

My heart is heavy, but I will find comfort
in You, Jesus. My hope is in You. Please fill
my heart with Your love so I can face this
loss knowing that You are in control. You
conquered death and made a way for
me to be with You forever.

I will follow You, Lord. Even though I'm sad right now, I know that You have a plan for my good. I will rejoice in Your saving grace and Your holy name. Please give me and my family peace during this hard time. Thank You for Your mercy and Your love.

Choosing between What's Easy and What's Right

*The precepts of the LORD are right, giving joy
to the heart. The commands of the LORD
are radiant, giving light to the eyes.*
PSALM 19:8

. . . .

Just because something is easy, doesn't make it right. Sometimes choosing to do the right thing is hard, but it always honors God. As His child, you are a light in the world and your choices are an important part of your daily walk with Him.

The Lord spoke to the prophet Jeremiah and said, "Stand at the crossroads and look; ask for the ancient paths, ask where the good way is, and walk in it, and you will find rest for your souls" (6:16). Let this verse remind your heart that true peace doesn't come from easy decisions but by seeking God's will for your life.

When you're faced with making a hard choice, pray, and ask God to direct your steps. Think about Jesus and all the hard decisions He made to take up His cross. He loves you and will never let you down.

Lord, You know where I stand. Please teach me what the right choice is. Show me mercy, and give me the strength to make the right decision. Your ways are perfect.

Give me the courage, God, to choose the right thing. Even when it's a hard choice, give me peace and wisdom to grow in righteousness. I know You want what's best for me, so I ask You to help me through this difficult moment of having to choose.

Lord, I'm constantly tempted to pick what's easy. All around me, people pick the things that are easy to deal with and fun. Please help me remember that I'm here to do Your will. Thank You for showing me the right way to go.

God Seems Silent

Even though I walk through the darkest valley,
I will fear no evil, for you are with me;
your rod and your staff, they comfort me.
PSALM 23:4

The enemy wants you to believe that God leaves His people alone. He wants you to believe that God doesn't love you anymore and that you aren't worthy of God's love. But the truth is, God thinks you're amazing, and there's nothing He won't do to keep you close to His heart.

There was a man named Elijah in the Old Testament who loved God and wanted to tell everyone about His mighty name. As a prophet, Elijah encountered a lot of people who didn't want to hear his messages about God. They even tried to take Elijah's life.

This made the prophet sad and he ran away, but God loved him like He loves you. He met with Elijah. The Bible says God came to him in a gentle whisper (1 Kings 19:12). So, when it seems like life is full of distractions and God is silent, remember Elijah and how God met with him in the silence.

God, please let me know You're here.
Right now it feels like You're far away,
but I know the truth. The truth is, You
are carrying me through this tough time.
Speak to me, and help me hear the
gentle whisper of Your sweet voice.

Lord, I know that You are leading me.
I know that You are holding me close and
that You are my shield. Thank You for loving
me! No matter what I feel today, please
remind me that You are here with me. Lord,
I know that You don't leave me alone.
I praise Your holy name!

Show me how to grow closer to You in the quiet times. Strengthen my faith so I will lean in and stay close to Your plans for me. Guide me through my Bible, and teach me to trust You more. When I get distracted, please show me how to concentrate on Your love.

I Don't Feel Good

*But he said to me, "My grace is sufficient for
you, for my power is made perfect in weakness."*
2 CORINTHIANS 12:9

. . . .

Days come when you don't feel good. Maybe
it's because you're sick, or maybe you feel run
down and just need a good nap. Sometimes you
may not feel good because you're sad. Perhaps
you've felt like God is far away and can't hear
your prayers.

The apostle Paul experienced all of these emotions. He was really sad, but at his lowest he discovered that God's grace was all he needed. He went on to say that the Lord's power is made strong in our weakness. Hebrews 4:16 says, "Let us then approach God's throne of grace with confidence, so that we may receive mercy and find grace to help us in our time of need."

Focus on the facts. Jesus loves you, and He has not left you alone. Lift up your heart to Him, and keep praying. Don't stop. He hears every word. Feel Him hold you close. He is mercy and grace, and He thinks you're wonderful!

Please help me know You are near, Father God. Remind me that I matter to You, no matter what I'm feeling. No matter what the enemy tries to throw at me, You are almighty, and You care for me. Thank You for loving me through the hard times. Thank You for being my shield.

Jesus, thank You for coming down from heaven to rescue me. Show me how to wait on You and listen for Your voice. Speak to me. Tell me everything You have planned for me, and give me the strength to do Your will.

Lord, Your ways are perfect.
Guide me down the right path.
Lead me by Your mercy and grace.
When the day feels too hard to
handle, remind me that
You are bigger than my struggles.
Jesus, please keep my eyes on
You. Show me how much You
love me. I love You, Jesus!

Someone I Know Is Sick

Surely he took up our pain
and bore our suffering.
Isaiah 53:4

. . . .

When someone close to you is sick, you want them to feel better, but your worries might grow if they don't get better right away. God, however, is with you, and He is with your friend who doesn't feel good. In His Word, God reminds you that Jesus takes up your sickness and your pain.

Use times of sickness to pray for your friend and get closer to God. Be an encouragement and listen for God to show you ways to be a blessing. Just letting your friend know you're praying for them will lift their spirits.

Jesus cared about His friends when they were sick, too. The Bible mentions that Jesus went into his disciple Peter's house and healed Peter's mother-in-law, who was really sick with a bad fever. Matthew 8:15 says, "He touched her hand and the fever left her." Jesus is the Great Healer, and He will take care of you and your friends, too.

Lord, I pray that You will help my friend
feel better. I pray that You will use me to
make them smile during this time of hurting.
Thank You for showing me in Your Word
that You heal and that You care about
everything that bothers us.

God, I want to be honest and tell You that
sometimes I don't understand things.
I don't know why my friend is sick, but I
praise You for loving us. I praise You for all
the blessings You shower over us. I pray
for my friend and ask that You would bless
them and help them feel better soon.

I hope my friend feels better. I don't feel good when I think about how they hurt inside. Please watch over them and let them know You're there with them. Jesus, I pray that You would lead me closer to You as I pray for my sick friend.

No One Understands

*May the God of hope fill you will all joy and peace
as you trust in him, so that you may overflow
with hope by the power of the Holy Spirit.*
ROMANS 15:13

· ·

One of the great Hebrew names of God is Jehovah-Jireh. This translates as "God who provides." Plant this powerful truth deep in your heart. When it feels like no one truly understands what you're feeling or what you're going through, God does. He sees every part of your life. Don't ever forget that He made you special.

God isn't bound by time. He is outside of it, so He can look ahead and see every day that you will have before you even see tomorrow. This means, as your Provider, He sees every one of your needs before they arise. He is also filling your heart with His hope so you will be delivered from your current struggles.

Two great passages to consider are Genesis 22:13–14 and Philippians 4:19. In both, you can see that God does understand. And remember that not only does He understand, but He also provides everything you need!

Lord, forgive me. I'm easily distracted by the disappointments in life. I pray that You'd fill my heart with more of Your love and truth. Remind me that You alone are my provider of everything I need. Remind me that, in You, my life is complete.

Thank You for giving me the gift of life. Thank You for Your promise to always watch over me. Your words are true, and I ask You to help me. Help me focus on Your plans. I want to follow You, but sometimes I feel disappointed when things don't work out the way I thought they should. Jesus, I know there were times when You felt disappointed.

Please guide me through the pages of my Bible, and help me learn how You handled the hurtful times. Thank You for being my King. Thank You for never leaving me alone and for giving me hope!

Being Disappointed

Above all, love each other deeply,
because love covers over a multitude of sins.
1 Peter 4:8

. . . .

There are times when you feel disappointed because other people hurt your feelings. You might be expecting something to happen a certain way and when it doesn't, disappointment comes, unwelcome and unwanted. Don't let the disappointments get you down. Don't let them define you.

Let God know what hurts your heart. He is big enough to help carry you through the times when nothing seems to be going right. God was also called El Shaddai, the All Sufficient God. In Genesis 17:1, God tells Abraham that He is almighty. Nothing is too hard for our great God.

When it seems like you're stuck in a situation that isn't getting better, call out to the One who is mighty enough to solve it. Call out to God, and tell Him what hurts you. Ask Him to fill your heart and take away your burden. He is there for you. He loves you because you are His!

Lord, I pray that You will help me make
sense of this disappointment. I feel let
down because of someone else's actions.
Please help me know that my identity is in
You alone. Help me do what Jesus did and
love anyway. Instead of living in a place of
hurt, give me strength to love others like
You teach me in Your Word.

Jesus, help me not to have any expectations
when I think about the people in my life.
You are the best promise keeper, so please
remind me of all the ways You fill my heart.
Show me how to live my days by Your
courage. Teach me how to care for
those who let me down.

Jesus, the disappointments of life
make me feel unwanted and alone,
but I know that You are with me.
Show me how to live my life for You.

FEAR OF FAILING

*Trust in the LORD with all your heart and
lean not on your own understanding; in all
your ways submit to him, and he will
make your paths straight.*
PROVERBS 3:5-6

. . . .

The first step in not fearing failure is to trust
God with everything that's in you. When you
allow yourself to make this change, making
mistakes won't mean you are a mistake. The
enemy wants you to believe that your mistakes
keep you away from God. Trust that God is
bigger than your mistakes.

Next, after you give God everything, it's important not to slip back into a routine of trying to figure out your situation. When you believe that God is in control, it won't matter if you have all the answers.

In everything you do, let God know how grateful you are for His grace. He promises to make your paths straight. When you are walking in God's plans, you can be confident that even though some things in life may be confusing, you know that Jesus is always for you.

Lord, I feel bad when I make mistakes, because I feel like I'm letting You down. Please forgive me, Jesus. Please fill my heart, and remind me that You are here. Show me places in Your Word where You take people and their mistakes and help them by Your mercy.

My heart is heavy sometimes because I try to do the right thing but mess up. I get afraid of doing the wrong thing. I don't want to let You down. Please forgive me, and show me how to live a life that is pleasing to You. I love You, Lord. Thank You for saving me!

God, You are good. All the time,
You care about me and hold me
through the ups and downs of
life. Take my mistakes, and help
me become humble knowing that
You forgive me. Show me that my
mistakes don't define me. Show me
how much I matter to You.

Teased because of My Looks

For you created my inmost being; you knit me together in my mother's womb. I praise you because I am fearfully and wonderfully made.
PSALM 139:13-14

God made you beautiful. He thinks you are wonderful in every way. Whether you are up or down, God knows what you're going through. He knows your thoughts and is there to help you sort them out. He won't leave you alone. You have been fearfully and wonderfully made.

Don't ever doubt God's love for you. You are His treasure. His hands guide you and hold you. Even though there might be some days when you don't think you measure up, His light shines over you. The Bible says that you were made in His image. Let that powerful truth grab hold of your heart and give you confidence.

Don't get down on yourself because of your looks. You are so special to God. Never forget this. He has wonderful plans for you that you cannot imagine. God doesn't make mistakes. He made you beautiful, and that's a fact!

There are many days I look in the mirror and don't like what I see. Please help me see myself the way You see me, God. Thank You for Your words that remind me how much You care for me. You are my Father, and I love You for giving me the gift of life.

Please help me, Jesus, to have confidence in the person You made me to be. Give me courage to know that in Your eyes I'm something special. Help me understand that Your hands have crafted something beautiful in me, so that I don't get caught up in the enemy's lies.

God, I'm sorry when I doubt Your promises. Please forgive me. Thank You for reminding me how special I am to You. Help me see all the ways You created me unique. Teach me all the ways You made me wonderful. Thank You, Jesus, for loving me.

Forgiveness

If we confess our sins, he is faithful and just
and will forgive us our sins and purify
us from all unrighteousness.
1 JOHN 1:9

. . . .

God is the One who made a way. He was the
One who sent His only Son to save you. Jesus
has rescued you. Don't let pride get in the way
of reaching out to Jesus. Call to Him, and tell
Him your mistakes. Listen to Him call you
forgiven. He gives His word that He is faithful
and will do this.

Cry out to God, and know that all your mistakes are forgiven. Nothing will ever come between you and the Lord. He protects you from evil and guards your heart from the enemy's plans. God is your strong foundation and your rock. He will never let you down.

Don't be ashamed. Don't let guilt keep you from running to God. Tell Him everything. He will use you to carry His light so that it shines in your life and over the people you will meet today.

Jesus, please forgive me. I feel like I keep making the same mistakes over and over again. Help me know that You died for all my mistakes—the ones I've made and the ones still to come. I don't want to let You down. I'm sorry.

I feel sad every time I make a mistake. Jesus, I'm asking for more of Your love right now. Show me the way. Thank You for taking up Your cross, which was really my cross—the burden of all my sins—and proving to me that I am truly loved by You.

I need You, Jesus. I need You to lift me up and hold me close to Your heart. I don't want to take You for granted. I don't want to be afraid to ask for forgiveness. Please help me get through this time. Lead me so that I may know I'm forgiven.

MY PARENTS ARE FIGHTING

"Do not let your hearts be troubled."
JOHN 14:1

• •

Please don't forget that God is your hiding place. Even though it's stressful when your parents argue, you are not alone to sort through all the emotions. Psalm 32:7 says that He will protect you from trouble and surround you with songs of deliverance. This means that even though it feels messy when your parents fight, your heavenly Father is protecting your heart.

Remember that God wants you to lean in close to Him. Pray for your parents. They love you, and God loves you more, so just know that you are not the reason for the argument. God is shielding you, and He keeps His word. He is faithful and will always guard your life.

The negative words and the disagreements that are spoken by your parents make you feel sad, but don't forget that your hope is in Jesus. Rely on Him to carry you through the stormy days when family members fight.

Lord, it makes me nervous when my parents argue. I pray for them. Protect all of us. Help them to love each other like You love us. Let me know that even though this is a difficult time, You are still in control and that You're never letting go of me.

I lift my parents up to You, Lord Jesus. Right now, I'm thinking about that time when You and the disciples were in that boat together. The storm was raging all around, but You were in charge of the wind and the waves. You calmed Your friends like You calmed the sea. Please do the same for me.

I pray for Your peace to fill our house, Lord. I pray that Your presence fills our hearts. I pray that You will help my parents stop arguing and that You will show them how to rely on Your love.

WHAT'S GOING ON?

For God is not a God of disorder but of peace.
1 CORINTHIANS 14:33

. . . .

God is in control! Even though life seems confusing, trust that He is holding you safe in His mighty arms. Don't feel weird—just cry out to Him, and tell Him everything you have to say. God is there to hear every one of your prayers. God knows that you're confused. He is not going to love you any less or leave you because you doubt.

God is there to protect you from the things that are making you sad. Proverbs 30:5 says, "Every word of God is flawless; he is a shield to those who take refuge in him." Keep reading your Bible! Let His words fill your heart.

God made you, and that means you are important. Listen to Him show you the way. He cares about you so much more than you'll ever know. Believe that He doesn't want you to spend all your time feeling frustrated. Use this time to rely on your Creator. He loves you!

God, I don't understand why some things happen the way they do. I know that You have good plans for me. I know You are the author of peace. Please fill my life with hope and love. Help me know that You are here guiding me through these confusing times.

Teach me Your plans for my life. Please give me strength to do Your will. I get confused because sometimes my days don't go like I think they should. Sometimes my heart is heavy because I feel like I'm doing everything right but things still go wrong. Be my guide. Take my hand, and show me where to go. Give me faith to follow You.

Lord, please just help me take a deep breath and rely on You for everything. I'm giving You all the confusing parts of my life and trusting that You will use them to draw me closer to Your loving heart.

MOVING

For we live by faith, not by sight.
2 CORINTHIANS 5:7

· ·

Moving and having to be the "new kid" is hard. Your whole world gets turned upside down, and it feels like God forgot about you. The exact opposite is true! The Bible is filled with people moving. In fact, many of those stories are of God commanding the people to move and the people having to put their faith in Him.

Noah was a man who lived in a time when it never rained, but God came to him and told him to build the ark. Can you imagine all the crazy feelings Noah must have felt? He didn't know the outcome, but the important thing with the move was that he trusted God. And then there was Abraham. The Lord told him to leave everything behind and go to a faraway land, and Abraham obeyed.

Trust God, and keep your faith in Him. The move you're about to make will be okay. He has great plans for you!

Jesus, You know I'm scared and that I really don't want to move. I'm afraid because I don't know what's coming. All my friends are here. My school. My teachers. Please fill my heart with hope, and help me keep my faith in all Your plans for me.

God, please show me more stories in Your Word where people had to move. Teach me how to have an obedient heart. I want to glorify You and not complain. You are holy, and You've never let me down. Guide my thoughts so I can stay confident in Your promises during this time of uncertainty.

Lord, my prayer is that You will take
this move and lead me closer to You.
I would rather stay, but I believe You
are working behind the scenes. I will
trust You and make the best of things!

MY FRIEND IS GOING THROUGH HARD TIMES

No one should seek their own good,
but the good of others.
1 CORINTHIANS 10:24

Maybe you have a friend who's going through a hard time but you don't know how to help. Maybe you don't have the right words to say. Just being there for your friend who's hurting is enough. Just letting them know you care will help them know that God cares for them, too.

Remind your friend to read the Bible. Remind them that God is a promise keeper and that He fills your friend's heart with His love. You can even read the same passage as your friend and share all the ways God speaks to you about His Word. Encourage your friend who is hurting with the truth that God's love is never ending.

Even though the enemy seeks to steal your friend's hope, tell them the truth. Tell them that God's desire is to shower them with grace. Tell them that Jesus is their Living Water and that He is enough to get through every hard time.

I'm sad to see my friend hurting. I wish there was a way I could make their trouble go away, but I am relying on You, God, to help them. Fill their heart with Your hope. Tell them that everything will be okay. I pray that You will be their strength.

I know what it's like to carry the heavy weight of sadness. Please lift that burden off my friend today. Thank You, Lord, for walking by their side and holding their hand. You are a wonderful God who cares. I lift my friend up to You and pray that You will take away all the things that are causing them pain.

Lord, I'm asking that You will help my friend deal with all the things that are hurting them. I praise You for caring about all of us. Have mercy on my friend. Please let them know that You are taking care of all their burdens.

Making BIG Mistakes

As far as the east is from the west, so far has he removed our transgressions from us.
PSALM 103:12

. . . .

Don't let your mistakes pull you away from God. That's what the enemy wants. When you accepted Jesus as your Savior, your heart was made clean, once and for all. You are eternally forgiven. The enemy wants to attack your feelings so you will start to believe that God only cares about you some of the time.

The truth is, even when you make big mistakes, God still loves you and He still calls you His beloved child. That's because the power of the cross and what Jesus did for you never fails or fades. Confess your sins. Humble yourself before God, and ask Him to forgive you. Let Him be in charge of everything.

Rely on God. He is strong and will help you overcome your problems. He is your Protector and you will always be special to Him. See God go before you today. Follow Him because He is always worthy.

Lord, please forgive me. I feel bad for the big mistakes I made. I don't want to mess up. I feel the shame that comes from going against Your commands. Please forgive me, and let me know I still matter to You. Thank You, Jesus, for the cross!

God, I'm so sorry for doing the wrong things. I'm sorry that I keep messing up. I praise You for reminding me that no matter what happens You still love me. I need that truth so much. I praise You for Jesus! I praise You for never letting go of me!

I am so sorry for disobeying You.
I want to do the right thing every
time. I'm sorry for the times I've
been selfish and gone against You.
Please help me do the right thing.
Help me obey all Your commands.
I want to keep becoming the person
You made me to be. I love You.

My Pet Died

Are not five sparrows sold for two pennies?
Yet not one of them is forgotten by God.
LUKE 12:6

. . . .

God cares about you so much. He knows how much you are hurting because of the loss of your pet. Animals are very special to God because He created them. The Bible even shows that animals are important. In 2 Samuel 12:1–6, you can read how King David became upset when he heard how a pet lamb was stolen from its owner. In the Gospel of Luke, you can read how Jesus said that not one sparrow is forgotten by God. Psalm 50:10 reminds you that every animal belongs to God.

Know that God is with you during this time of sadness. Rely on Him to be your strength. Talk to God and let Him know everything you're feeling. He loves you. Do the same with your parents. They love you. Don't keep your feelings in. Remember the fun times you had with your pet. God is holding you close, and He is strong enough to get you through this difficult time.

God, I miss my pet so much. It hurts to think about it. Please help me get through this. It's hard to think about anything else. Remind me that You love me and that I'm not alone right now. Remind me that You are here with me in this sad time.

Jesus, I need You. My feelings are crazy, and I can't think straight. Help me read my Bible so I can be reminded of all the ways You love and care about me. Remind me of Your plans for my life, and comfort me. I miss my pet, but help me to move on.

Please help me, Lord. I can't get through this without You. Please be my hope. Show me how to take the next step. You made me, and I still know that You have good plans for me. I praise You for today. Help me during this really hard time.

My Friends Are Bad Influences

Submit yourselves, then, to God.
Resist the devil, and he will flee from you.
JAMES 4:7

. . . .

It can be very hard to walk away from friends who always make bad choices. You don't want to lose friends or have people make fun of you. But the truth is, you have to focus on the fact that you are God's chosen child, dearly loved and forever forgiven. You have been set free! You don't have to worry about what others think about you, because Jesus thinks you're wonderful.

When your friends become bad influences, remember that Jesus is with you to be your strength. By His glorious power, you will break the enemy's temptations that he throws at you. Tell God that you are giving Him the stressful situation with your friends, and don't doubt that He will take care of you.

Use this time to be a light. Others are watching. Instead of worrying, go and give care and compassion to someone who is hurting. Let each one of your words and actions celebrate your Savior! Jesus will make your enemy flee.

God, it doesn't seem like things will ever change. I believe You are with me, but the situation with my friends is hard. They keep doing the wrong things, but I don't want them to think I'm a tattletale. I don't want them to think I'm better than they are. Please show me ways I can stand up for what's right.

Right now, Lord Jesus, I'm giving You this stressful situation with my friends. Hold me, Lord. Take this, and keep me safe by the power of Your mercy and grace. I know You are stronger than the things that tempt me. Father, show me the way out of this.

Jesus, speak words of courage over
me. Say the word and it will be done.
Thank You for the cross. Thank You
for helping me walk away from bad
situations. Show me the way to
integrity, and help me follow You.

My Friend Doesn't Know Jesus

For it is with your heart that you believe and are justified, and it is with your mouth that you profess your faith and are saved.
ROMANS 10:10

. . . .

If your friend doesn't know Jesus, you have a wonderful opportunity to share the Gospel message. You have the chance to lead your friend to the cross of Jesus! There are four Bible verses that you can use as you share:

- "For all have sinned and fall short of the glory of God." (Romans 3:23)
- "For the wages of sin is death, but the gift of God is eternal life in Christ Jesus our Lord." (Romans 6:23)

- "But God demonstrates his own love for us in this: While we were still sinners, Christ died for us." (Romans 5:8)
- "For it is with your heart that you believe and are justified, and it is with your mouth that you profess your faith and are saved." (Romans 10:10)

Use these as your guide. Pray for your friend's heart. This is a very special chance you have to be a witness for Jesus. Rejoice that He is using you to share the Good News!

Lord, my friend doesn't know You. Give me a humble spirit to share the Gospel and share Your gift of salvation with them. Let me speak in grace so they will know I really care about their heart. I pray that they will listen and hear truth. I pray that You will save them.

Jesus, my friend is hurting. They are wondering what to do. I know they need You. I pray for the right words. I pray that Your Holy Spirit will give me boldness to speak Your truth in love. Thank You for this special chance to tell my friend about You and what You did for them.

God, I'm so thankful that You have made this day for me. Thank You for letting me be a special part of Your kingdom plans to lead my friend to the cross. Please use me for Your glory. Save my friend by Your mighty power.

I Feel Helpless

" 'If you can'?" said Jesus. "Everything
is possible for one who believes."
MARK 9:23

. . . .

God loves you. The heart of His sweet Son
beats for you. His desire for you is so powerful
that no sad day can pull you away from Him.
Your heavenly Father's mercy surrounds you
and heals you from the things that have made
you feel helpless.

God understands. He knows that you are
feeling like nothing is going right. He knows
that you feel like nothing you do matters. He
knows what it feels like because He watched
Jesus take on the sins of the world. He knows
because He saw the soldiers mock His Son
and spit on Him. He saw them taunt Him
with the crown of thorns.

God wanted to save Jesus from this darkness, but He also wanted to save you. So when your day is covered with hurt and your heart aches, cry out to God and know without doubting that He hears you and is there to help. Every time!

I feel so helpless, Lord. I'm sad because everything I try to do isn't working out.

I know that You care about all of me, so right now, I'm giving You everything—

every hurt, every hope, every part of me. Please take them and be my helper.

Take over, and lead me in Your will.

God, I'm slowly understanding that You want what's best for me. I'm starting to realize that You are the One who cares about me more than anyone else does. Strengthen my faith so I may follow You closely. Please help me.

Thank You, Jesus, for reminding me that in You everything is possible. Help me walk away from the doubts and run after You. Help me know that You love me even though I keep messing up.

Thank You for giving me a purpose. Help me trust that Your ways and Your words are perfect. Thank You for caring!

OBEYING MY PARENTS AND TEACHERS

Children, obey your parents
in the Lord, for this is right.
EPHESIANS 6:1

Obedience is a common theme in the Bible. In the beginning of Genesis, you'll find God telling Adam and Eve not to eat off the tree of knowledge. A few chapters later, there's Noah and the Ark. In Genesis 12, God tells Abraham to pick up all his possessions and family and move.

Fast-forward to the New Testament, and the same desire for obedient hearts is there. Jesus obeyed the Father, and you, too, are being called to the same command: "Children, obey your parents in everything, for this pleases the Lord" (Colossians 3:20). God made you to have an obedient and teachable spirit.

Even on the hard days, remember that obeying your parents and teachers honors God. James 1:25 says, "Whoever looks intently into the perfect law that gives freedom, and continues in it—not forgetting what they have heard, but doing it—they will be blessed in what they do." You are loved, and your Creator will give you the strength to obey.

God, I want to tell You how grateful I am for Your Word. I'm so thankful I have my Bible. Teach me through it. Remind me of all the times Your children were obedient and You were honored. It's hard sometimes because I don't like being told what to do.

Help me be more like Jesus. I want to obey my parents and teachers. I pray for stronger faith so that in all situations, I can feel Your peace. Help me to live out all Your commands. I want to be an example to my friends. I want them to know You because of my life.

Give me the courage to do what the
Bible says. I pray for more grace and
mercy. Help me be a good listener
and follow everything You ask of
me. Thank You for my life.

Money

*But seek first his kingdom and his
righteousness, and all these things
will be given to you as well.*
MATTHEW 6:33

. . . .

When your family has money problems, it can
feel embarrassing. Your friends buy new clothes
and toys, but you're left with all the old things.
But God promises that He is taking care of you.

Pray for the strength not to worry about
the things you don't have. Pray for the faith not
to worry about things you think you should
have. God cares about you and will provide
everything you need.

Even when it seems like nothing will ever get better, God's love for you is greater still. The enemy will try to make you feel that your worth is linked to money. He says that nothing will ever change if your family has money problems. He spins his lies in hopes that you will spend your day worrying about things that are out of your control.

Let God carry you. Let Him protect you through every storm. He knows and will provide everything you need. Rely on Him!

Lord, I don't want to be selfish; I want to be grateful for everything You've done for me. I just want to be honest that it's really hard when money's tight. I hear my parents talking about being in debt, and I worry about the future. Please bless our family.

Jesus, You paid my greatest debt in full! Help me remember this when I start worrying about our money problems. Please help my heart focus on the truth of my salvation. Your beautiful cross reminds me how much I'm loved. Thank You for reminding me that everything is going to be okay.

My parents are working hard
to make ends meet. I wish
our money problems would go
away. Lord, forgive me for doubting
Your wonderful power. Please
take our financial burden and make
a way for my family to get through
this tough time. I pray that You will
help me focus on everything
You've done for me.

FIGHTING WITH SOMEONE

Be completely humble and gentle;
be patient, bearing with one another in love.
EPHESIANS 4:2

. . . .

Having an argument or a fight with someone doesn't feel good. It might make you confused and possibly even wonder where God is. The enemy wants you to believe the lie that if you are in a fight with someone, God has left you. That is simply not the truth.

The Bible is clear that nothing will ever be able to separate you from the love of Jesus! Nothing! Rest in that promise and pray for God to help you through this time of trials. God is not leaving you alone. Ask Him for wisdom, and listen for His voice.

Confess your mistakes if that is what led to the disagreement. Be humble, and don't let pride get in the way of restoring your friendships. Bring the love of Jesus into your relationship that is hurting, and pray that He will mend what is broken. You don't have to worry about defending yourself, because Jesus is your Defender.

Jesus, I'm having a fight with my friend, and it hurts. Please help me sort out my feelings. Show me where I went wrong, and give me the strength to admit my mistakes. I want to live the right way and have integrity. Show me how to make things right, and give me the courage to stick up for You.

I feel terrible that I let You down. The argument has been going on because I'm too prideful to say I was wrong. Lead me to Bible verses, and speak to me through them so my heart can be filled with Your truth and not my emotions.

Lord, I pray for my friend whom I've been fighting with. Bless them, please. Remind them how much You love them. I'm confused because I don't know how it all started, but You've given me Your word that, no matter what, You still love me.

DOUBTING MY FAITH

For God so loved the world that he gave his one and only Son, that whoever believes in him shall not perish but have eternal life.

JOHN 3:16

. . . .

God knows there are days when you feel like He's forgotten you. When the enemy says your faith is a waste of time, say, "Jesus is my Answer. He is all I need!" When it seems like the evil one is winning, you say, "Jesus has already won the battle for my heart!"

Trust God to strengthen your heart. He always keeps His eyes on you. He won't let your weak faith overcome you, because Jesus is the One who overcame death. Jesus is the One who paid the ultimate price for your heart. He suffered in your place because of love.

Through every situation you face today, trust God and His unfailing love. Trust Him, even in the hard times. Trust that He is holding you through every smile and every tear. Even when the hurting seems too hard to bear and your faith feels finished, never forget that God is never letting you go. Your heart is beautiful to Him.

God, thank You for reminding me that my salvation is secure. Forgive my weak faith. Help me remember that my mistakes can never undo what Jesus did for me on the cross. Praise Your holy name for that truth. I want to be strong, but I have all these thoughts that try to break my faith.

I'm sorry when I doubt. Please forgive me, Jesus. I want to face every day that You give me with rock-solid faith, but I always mess up and feel guilty. The guilt turns to shame, and my shame seems to pile up and smother my faith. Please erase my shame by Your great love.

Lord, I don't want to take advantage of Your grace. Thank You for showing me that Your mercies are new every morning. I need Your mercy so badly. Please help me separate my emotions from Your truth so that I can move on with renewed faith in Your love for me.

BREAKING PROMISES

I will not violate my covenant
or alter what my lips have uttered.
PSALM 89:34

. . . .

God keeps His promises. He won't let you down. There's nothing to fear, because God goes before you, and He knows exactly what you need. Remember this when you're in a situation where a close friend breaks a promise. God knows you feel hurt and let down, but He won't leave you that way.

When a friend goes back on a promise, make sure that you keep God first. Don't let your friend's actions make you see your heavenly Father differently. The world is full of mistake-makers who make promises they don't keep. Use this time to learn more about God's character.

There may even come a time when you are the one to break a promise. Ask God to forgive your mistake, and make sure you apologize to the person you made the promise to. Pray that God gives you the courage to be a person of your word. Read His words in your Bible, and live out His commands. That's the way to stay anchored to truth and avoid breaking promises.

Lord, please help me sort out my feelings. I'm confused because my friend broke a promise, and I feel hurt. Remind me that Your love for me is never ending and that the plans You have for me won't be diminished because of my friend's mistake.

Father, thank You for listening to me. Thank You for caring about everything that I care about. Help me to remember that my identity is in Jesus and not in my friends. I pray for confidence to be a light for You. I pray for peace to bring to my friend who broke a promise. Thank You for being with me through all of this.

God, You are the great promise keeper. I pray that my life would reflect the trustworthiness of You to my friend, who didn't keep their word. Help me stay connected to You through this trying time.

LAZINESS

We do not want you to become lazy,
but to imitate those who through faith and
patience inherit what has been promised.
HEBREWS 6:12

. . . .

Jesus is with you. The Bible says in Psalm 68:35 that God gives you His power and strength. Let that truth move you away from laziness and spur you on to do great things for God. Pray for courage and for His will to be done, and move in the direction He leads.

Colossians 3:17 says, "Whatever you do, whether in word or deed, do it all in the name of the Lord Jesus, giving thanks to God the Father through him." Let this verse be your new motto. You were created for a great purpose. There is no one in the world like you. Use your position as a chosen child of God to tell the world about Jesus.

When you're tempted to give in to laziness, stand on the promise of your heavenly Father. Rise above the temptation to not work hard, and become all that God made you to be. Become a force for His holy name!

Lord, I need help. It's so easy to give in to laziness. I haven't been thinking about how special You made me. To be honest, I don't feel important, and most days I don't feel like I matter too much. Forgive me. Help me rediscover my real worth in You.

After spending time with You, I feel ashamed that I've been so lazy. I'm slowly realizing that this isn't who You made me to be. Help me be more like Jesus. Change my heart. Use my hands and feet for Your purposes. Give me a spirit of bravery to step up and work hard.

Jesus, I don't want to be lazy anymore. I want every one of my days—days that You have gifted me—to reflect who You are and what You've done for me. I want my actions to show my family and friends that You are where my motivation and strength come from. I love You!

I Don't Feel Loved

Let the morning bring me word of your unfailing love, for I have put my trust in you. Show me the way I should go, for to you I entrust my life.

PSALM 143:8

. . . .

God loves you. He is keeping your life safe in His mighty hands. When the enemy lurks around trying to plant lies in your heart, He is there to thwart his wicked plans. When the world wears you down with stress, God is there to hold you in the refuge of His strong arms.

Concentrate on trusting Him more today for everything you need. He loves you so much that He gave you Jesus. Think about Him all day long. Get to the place where He is all you want, because He alone is all you need. Jesus shed His blood to pay the debt you could never afford from your own resources, so rejoice!

God loves you so much. He is your Provider. He is enough to sustain you. He has made your salvation secure. He has done these things because you are His precious child and He loves you!

Lord, I want to pray 1 John 4:16 over my life today. "And so we know and rely on the love God has for us. God is love. Whoever lives in love lives in God, and God in them." Help me to know Your love for me is real. Help me to live my life right in the center of it.

God, I also pray Romans 8:39 to be planted in my heart. "Neither height nor depth, nor anything else in all creation, will be able to separate us from the love of God that is in Christ Jesus our Lord." Help me remember this all day long. Thank You for this truth!

Jesus, I lift up the words of Romans 5:5. "And hope does not put us to shame, because God's love has been poured out into our hearts through the Holy Spirit, who has been given to us." Thank You for doing this for me. Thank You for caring this much about me!

Low Self-Esteem

Don't let anyone look down on you because you are young, but set an example for the believers in speech, in conduct, in love, in faith and in purity.
1 Timothy 4:12

· ·

When you start feeling sad or begin battling low self-esteem, remember that your life isn't a random set of hours but a secure set of places God has established for you (Psalm 16). Follow Him to these pastures and rejoice in the fact that the Creator keeps your days safe in His loving arms.

This new day is for you to keep your eyes on God and not on your circumstances. Let His love and strength remind you how much you're worth. He is always by your side. Receive His grace in every moment so your heart is always glad! Constantly celebrate all the blessings He has given you.

Most of all, God is never going to abandon you. Remain close to Him, and know that eternal peace is found in Him. Let God show you His plans for your life. He loves you!

God, for some reason I feel sad. I'm having a hard time feeling good about myself. Forgive me, because I know this goes against everything the Bible teaches. Help me see myself the way You do. Help me study more of Your Word, which says I was made special and with an important purpose.

God, thank You for being patient with me. Thank You for calling me Your child. That's something I can't believe because of all the mistakes I make, but I do believe it's true. Thank You for sending Jesus to save me and making all this possible.

Lord, I pray that You would give me the courage I need to look in the mirror and see what You see. I pray that You would replace my low self-esteem with Your truth about my real identity in Jesus. Thank You for loving me and never letting me go!

I'm Angry

*Everyone should be quick to listen,
slow to speak and slow to become angry.*
JAMES 1:19

. . . .

You don't have to worry about defending your-self. That's God's specialty! The Bible says that He is your Defender. There is never a time when He is not looking out for you. Getting angry is a defense mechanism that seems appropriate when another person says or does something to us that harms our thoughts or bodies. But the book of James goes on to say that human anger does not produce the righteousness that God desires (1:20).

Getting angry might feel right for the moment, but it doesn't allow you to be humble. Trust God to keep planting His commands in your heart. Colossians 3:8 says to rid yourself of anger. Erase that coping strategy, or way of dealing with your circumstances, and begin to rely on your heavenly Father to guard your life.

Pray for the Lord to replace the bitter seeds of anger with seeds of His everlasting peace. Follow Jesus, your Prince of Peace (Isaiah 9:6), and let Him calm your heart so you can walk away from anger.

Lord, I pray Isaiah 26:3 over my life today: "You will keep in perfect peace those whose minds are steadfast, because they trust in you." I trust that You will do this for me. I ask that You will keep Your peace surrounding me as I work on not responding in anger.

God, I also pray that You would help me keep the words of Jesus in Matthew 5:9 close to my heart: "Blessed are the peacemakers, for they will be called children of God." Help me be known to my family and friends as one who stood for peace.

Second Thessalonians 3:16 says,
"Now may the Lord of peace himself
give you peace at all times and in every
way. The Lord be with all of you."
Be with me, God. When the stressful
situations come, help me to draw from
the wells of Your peace and respond
in the right manner.

BEING AFRAID

"The Lord is my helper; I will not be afraid.
What can mere mortals do to me?"
HEBREWS 13:6

. . . .

Jesus told His friends not to be afraid. He told them to get courage from Him and not fear the things in life that seemed too big and scary to overcome (Matthew 14:27).

With Jesus, this kind of fearless living is for you, too! Hear His sweet voice comfort your nervous heart as He says you are worth more than anything, and because of that, He will take care of you (Matthew 10:31). Follow Him. When His friends were afraid to leave everything behind, Jesus said not to worry because He was with them (Luke 5:10).

Jesus is stronger and bigger than anything in your life that would cause you to worry. He is smarter and mightier than any force that might get in your way of following Him. He loves you and wants you to be free from fear. Trust His promise to always take care of you. Lord, thank You for making me.

Help me to rely on Your Word that says You will always be there for me. Help me hear Jesus tell me not to be afraid. I want to put down my fears and reach out with empty hands and grab hold of Jesus.

Sometimes it seems hard not to worry, but I know that being afraid means I'm not trusting You. Forgive me, Jesus. Give me the courage and strength to keep my eyes on You and follow You wherever You lead me. Your ways are the only ones I want to walk in today.

God, I'm sorry that most days when
something stressful happens, my
first reaction is to be afraid. After
spending time in Your Word,
I see that this isn't what You desire.
I'm slowly understanding that You
have given me a spirit of life. Help
me grow into the courageous person
You see and made me to be.

I'M OVERWHELMED

*"Do not let your hearts be
troubled and do not be afraid."*
JOHN 14:27

· ·

Take a breath. It's going to be okay. If you feel
overwhelmed, don't worry because you are not
alone. Remember that your life is in God's
hands. He will not let you be shaken. Breathe
in the truth that God covers every one of your
days in His mercy and grace.

Jesus told His friends, "But the Advocate, the Holy Spirit, whom the Father will send in my name, will teach you all things and will remind you of everything I have said to you. Peace I leave with you; my peace I give you. I do not give to you as the world gives. Do not let your hearts be troubled and do not be afraid" (John 14:26–27). Be confident that your circumstance will not keep you down. You have the Holy Spirit and the peace of Jesus to keep you calm. You matter. Just keep your eyes on Jesus.

Take another breath and think about all the ways God has blessed you. You are special, and He loves you very much.

Right now I feel very overwhelmed and I'm just not sure how to pray. I want to be obedient and trust in Your promises, but it's hard because I feel worn down. Jesus, please help me keep my eyes on You. I know You are big enough to get me through this!

God, thank You for saving me. In the middle of these crazy feelings of stress, I know that You are with me. I can't take another step without You. But I pray that my feet run after You. I pray that I won't stop following You and all the wonderful plans You have made for me. I love You, Jesus.

I'm glad that You are a God who saves. I'm glad You care and always show me the truth about how much You love me. Please be with me. Please help me get through this stressful time.

FEELING UNSAFE

God is our refuge and strength,
an ever-present help in trouble.
PSALM 46:1

· ·

There are a lot of things you see and hear on TV, radio, and the Internet. Things like war and terrorism, crime and violence. Although these are very serious topics, they don't have to scare you, because you have the God of angel armies defending you (Psalm 89)! Stay rooted in God's Word, and listen to His voice.

You have been saved by the blood of Jesus, so there is nothing for you to worry about. He is with you all day, every day. He will protect you, and He will never leave you alone. The enemy wants you to focus on all the stressful things of the world. He wants you to feel unsafe. But hear Jesus call your name and say, "Don't be afraid."

This new day that the Lord has given is for trusting Him and all His promises. Follow Him, and know that He is with you always!

Lord, it's scary sometimes to hear about all the bad things that are happening in the world. Please keep me and my family safe. I'm so thankful for the Bible that reminds me You are the God of angel armies. There's nothing that can stop Your love for me.

God, most days it seems that I see something on the news that makes me nervous. I see things that are disturbing, and it makes me start to wonder about my safety. Thank You for promising to never leave me. Thank You for being almighty and more powerful than any of the bad stuff in the world.

Lord Jesus, I praise You. I'm so thankful that You saved me. I'm thinking about how powerful You are and how You conquered death once and for all. I know there's nothing You can't do. Keep my heart filled with Your peace during these difficult times.

MAKING NEW FRIENDS

Instead, I have called you friends,
for everything that I learned from my
Father I have made known to you.
JOHN 15:15

· ·

Sometimes it feels like making new friends is hard and awkward. Maybe you just moved to a new city and the thought of going to a new school and starting all over is a heavy burden to bear. Or maybe it was your close friend who moved and now you feel all alone. Either way, it's all going to be okay.

The great news is that Jesus calls you His friend! Be confident that He is with you as you go to school today. He is with you all day long, so don't worry about trying to fit in or get attention. He loves you just the way you are, which is just the way He made you to be.

As you wait to meet a new friend, rely on God to bring that person into your life, and be patient. He has great plans for you. Wait on His perfect timing.

Jesus, I'm so thankful that You are my friend. That helps me know that I don't have to try to make friends with the wrong people. Knowing You care about me more than anything takes the pressure off me trying to fit in with the wrong group of kids.

Lord, I ask that You would help me make a new friend. I pray that You would bring someone into my life who will help me love You more. And God, if my new friend turns out not to be a believer in You, then I pray You give me strength to be a faithful witness and tell them about Jesus. I know that You provide everything I need. God, I ask that You would hear my prayer for a new friend.

It's hard for me to find the right
words to say sometimes. Being in
this new situation is hard.
Thank You for helping me connect
with my new friend.

Schoolwork

Cast all your anxiety on
him because he cares for you.
1 PETER 5:7

. . . .

Going to school isn't easy. You have to keep up with all those subjects like reading and math, plus the many extras like PE and computers. Then there's homework and everything else that gets added to keep you really busy. Having the right attitude will help organize all of these expectations and make each day doable.

The Bible says that God is ready and waiting for you to put all the things that make you anxious on Him because He cares. Think about your school day. Think about the work, and cast it on your heavenly Father who loves you very much. This means asking Him for help to do your best in every subject, and leaving the results to Him.

Also, believe that you are not just at your school to learn and play. God has you there for so much more. Try to do your best on all your assignments. Work hard. You are a special part of His plan at home and at school!

Doing schoolwork isn't easy. Trying to keep up with all of my teachers' expectations is difficult to manage. Please, Lord, help me to always do my best. Remind me that I'm being a light for You every time I work hard, and help me to not get lazy by putting work off until the last minute.

God, I'm tired. School wears me out, but I know that You are with me. So I pray now that You would give me the strength to work hard. Guide my thoughts so I can always do my best no matter what the assignment.

Open my eyes, Lord, so that whether
I'm at school or at home I see my
education in a whole new way. I
pray that You would help me see
my schoolwork as a way that You
are growing me into the person
You created me to be. Thank You for
the chance to receive an education.
Thank You for loving me.

I Feel Hopeless

So do not fear, for I am with you;
do not be dismayed, for I am your God.
ISAIAH 41:10

· ·

Stop carrying the weight of all your worries. The enemy wants you to feel hope*less*, but God wants you to feel hope*ful*. His Word says that He is with you and that He doesn't want you to waste time feeling sad, because He is your God! He personally cares about everything you care about!

Pick up the promises of your Almighty Creator. He has made a covenant with you. He vows to protect your heart and to strengthen and help you. You have Jesus, and He is never leaving you. Jesus is with you forever.

Jesus loves you, and you matter so much to Him. Go into this new day carrying the hope of Christ, not ever once doubting that Almighty God is holding you in His powerful hands. Use this hope that never ends as encouragement to know that God has special plans for you. Trust Him, for He is all good, all the time.

Lord, please teach me how to have greater faith in all of Your promises. I pray that You will help me to put down all my worries and just start trusting that You want what's best for my life. Please fill my heart with hope.

Thank You for caring about exactly what I'm going through. Thank You for calling me Your child. Thank You for giving me Jesus, my life and my hope. Thank You for promising me that my hope in You is eternal and will never fade.

Thank You, Lord, for giving me a
new day to live in Your presence.
I find relief in knowing that You
love me no matter what happens
or what I feel. I pray that I continue
to find comfort in the fact that
You are always with me.

I Feel Lonely

*I have been crucified with Christ and I
no longer live, but Christ lives in me.*
GALATIANS 2:20

. . . .

Remember that you are never alone. Jesus is always with you. The enemy is skilled at whispering lies and making you feel unworthy of Jesus' grace. The devil wants you to feel lonely and believe that you are a disappointment to God. But remember: You are not ignored. You are not forgotten. You are not a failure or a waste. You are not insignificant or helpless. You are not despised, and you certainly are not a mistake.

Your worth is found in truth, and the truth is you are wonderful. You are loved and completely forgiven of all your sins. You are free. You are powerful. God has filled you with His presence. You don't have to earn His favor. In His eyes, you are well known and adored. You are a success, and you are important to God. You are special. You are so significant and helpful. You are adored.

I feel lonely sometimes. And sometimes, no matter how many people are around me, Lord, I still feel like I'm alone. I know You're there. Help me feel Your presence, Jesus. Teach me that I never have to believe the enemy's lie that You might abandon me one day. Thank You, God, for being here with me.

God, if I forget that You are near and start to feel isolated, please rescue me from the feelings of loneliness. When the enemy says my mistakes have caused You to reject me, please speak Your truth back into my heart. Please comfort me despite my doubts.

Jesus, You are my sweet and loving
Savior. Please keep pouring Your grace
and mercy out over my life.
Let me know over and over that
You're with me and You care.
Forgive me for doubting this, Lord.
Thank You for being patient and
understanding. Thank You for holding
me close to Your beautiful heart.

DIVORCE

He took the children in his arms, placed his
hands on them and blessed them.
MARK 10:16

· ·

Jesus told His friends not to stand in the way
of letting the children come to Him. He loves
you so much. If your parents are going through
a divorce, your emotions can be all stirred up
and you might even feel that it's all your fault.
Please know that your parents love you very
much. Even though everything feels confusing,
Jesus hasn't left you. Use this time to get closer
to Him. He will walk through this with you.

God loves you very much. In that same passage in the Gospel of Mark, Jesus goes on to tell His friends that His kingdom belongs to people who have childlike faith, people who trust God for everything, no matter what their situations are like. Close your eyes and listen for Him calling you by name. Hear Him remind you that through the divorce and all the emotional times that go with it, He will hold you and never let you go.

Lord, what my parents are going through is scary. I can't stand to think of a day when all of us aren't in the same house anymore. I pray that You would bless them and help them love each other the way You love them. I hope they will work things out. Please help them.

Jesus, please protect our family. I don't know why my parents are fighting, but I pray that You would show them the way. Help them listen to Your truth, and guide them back to the place where they will see that Your plans are best. I ask that You would let them feel Your love in a new way.

Dear God, I can't imagine what will happen if my parents get divorced. I know that You are not shaken by this, but I pray that You would comfort us. Please guide me and my family through this time of uncertainty. I pray more than anything that Your will is done.

Cancer

Truly he is my rock and my salvation;
he is my fortress, I will not be shaken.
PSALM 62:6

. . . .

If you have a family member or friend with
cancer, you know how crazy the journey can be.
Maybe you've had to go to the hospital and see
the hurting and sickness firsthand. Or perhaps
you've just been praying for healing. Through
it all, remember that God is your Shepherd
and that He is also with your loved one who
is battling cancer. God is the One who will
renew their strength. The cancer is confusing,
but God isn't.

God will provide. He will be with you and your family and friends so you don't have to fear all the unknowns that cancer brings. God is there to bring all of you comfort that only He can bring. Feel Him rain down mercy and grace. The cancer is not strong enough to steal your hope.

Take a minute to think about how mighty God is. Consider how His hands hold you. Think about how He is using you to be a source of inspiration to your friend or family member who is going through cancer.

Lord, I pray for my friend who has cancer.
I don't get it, but I know You are in charge.
I pray Psalm 62 over them right now. Please
help their soul find rest in You alone. Help
them know You are there for them. Comfort
their heart with Your love. You are wonderful.
Thank You for being our awesome helper.

I pray for my friend with cancer, Jesus.
I pray that they will know all of their hope
comes from You. I pray that they know
without doubting that in this difficult time
You are their rock and fortress. Please remind
them that the cancer cannot shake You!

Jesus, please be with my friend who has cancer. I praise You for being their mighty rock and their refuge. I believe that the cancer is only a temporary affliction. Help us to trust that You are the answer. Thank You for hearing my prayer.

OUT OF CONTROL

"I have told you these things, so that in me you may have peace. In this world you will have trouble. But take heart! I have overcome the world."
JOHN 16:33

. . . .

God is in control. He has said in His Word that He is not a God of disorder. Let go of trying to control the outcomes of each of your days. Don't try reaching through all the chaos of each moment; instead let God reach out and lift you above the confusion.

From the Egyptian captivity to the lion's den, from the fiery furnace to the belly of the whale, to the stormy sea that Jesus walked on, God had complete control of each of these situations. None of them caught Him off guard. The Israelites were unchained; the lions' mouths were shut; the flames were frozen; and the sea was calmed down into a sheet of glass.

Your life matters to God just as much as the lives spoken of in the Bible. To God, you are amazing. To Him, you are worth it all. He will restore all the things in your life that seem out of control, and He will surround you with limitless peace and mercy.

Lord, I ask that You would please take control of my life. Help me see my days through Your mercy. Help me to stop and listen to Your teaching so my life will look the way You want it to look. Please keep being patient with me. I'm sorry for all the mistakes I make.

Heavenly Father, I pray that You use this new day to show me stories in the Bible where You stepped in and rescued people from situations that were out of control. I praise You for helping me understand that You are always here for me.

God, I need You. I need the strength to give You this day and all that will come from it. Please take it, and order my thoughts and steps. Please talk to me along the way, and show me what Your will is. You are my wonderful and holy Creator, and I love You.

DISCONNECTED FROM GOD

*"'For in him we live and
move and have our being.'"*
ACTS 17:28

. . . .

If you feel far away from God, first understand
that He is not far away from you. Make sure that
you find a way to reconnect to Him through a
daily quiet time. Unplug the electronics and just
sit in His presence. Let all of life's distractions
go away, and lean in and listen. Hear Him speak
through His Word to you.

God desires a relationship with you. He thinks you're very special, and He has great things in store for your life. Don't miss out on a great adventure with Jesus just because you want to fill every moment of free time with games and friends and phone calls.

Take time to walk with the One who loves you. Take time to rediscover His beautiful truths in your Bible. Soak up all His promises, and let Him lead you to a deeper knowledge of His love for you.

God, please remind me that You're not far away. Help me to unplug from all the things that distract me, and let me reconnect with You. I confess that my daily routine is filled with activities that don't bring me closer to You, and I've been missing Your goodness.

Show me how to plug in to Your grace. Jesus, I pray right now for more faith to believe that Your will for me is best. Help me take daily quiet times with You so I can be renewed. Lead me and give me wisdom to discern what routines I should keep and which ones I should get rid of so I can fully connect to You.

For everything You've given me,
God, I praise Your mighty name.
For everything I've done to
take Your blessings for granted,
please forgive me. Bring me back
to the place where You and I are
fully connected and my heart
only wants to beat for You.

NEED MY INDEPENDENCE

*"Let the little children come to me,
and do not hinder them, for the kingdom
of God belongs to such as these."*
LUKE 18:16

' '

It's not wrong if you feel the desire to be independent. God made you different from anyone else He created. Out of all the people in the world, God lovingly made only one you. Think about that for a while, and let the reality of just how special you are soak in.

Being independent and becoming the person God made you to be doesn't mean you should disobey your parents and teachers. For a reason, the Lord has put those adults in your life to raise you up and give you important lessons as you mature.

Remember that Jesus called the children to Himself and told the people standing around not to hinder them. Jesus was saying not to let anything get in your way of having a relationship with Him. As you spend each day learning more about Him and all the ways He's made you unique, strive to depend on Jesus for everything. Praise His holy name for calling you His precious child!

Lord, as I grow closer to You each day, I feel the urge to become more of my own person. Help me understand this desire to be independent. I don't want this to stir up selfishness in my heart, but I want to understand all the ways You made me different. Knowing that being independent means learning how You made me unique is a blessing, and I'm grateful.

As I grow in an understanding of Your will for my life, help me to stay obedient to my parents and teachers. Please help me keep learning from them.

Jesus, hold me close. Call to me,
and I will follow You. I pray that
my relationship with You would not
depend on anyone or anything.
I'm thankful for our time together.
Thank You for bringing me into
Your arms and teaching me.

Injustice

For the LORD is a God of justice.
Blessed are all who wait for him!
ISAIAH 30:18

Most days, you will likely hear about many things that are happening in the world that don't seem fair. It all seems confusing because certain people win and other people look like they're losing out to injustice.

But the Bible is clear that God is the ultimate Judge of heaven and earth (Psalm 7:8). He is the One who will make everything work out for good. He protects His people. Even if this day doesn't bring immediate answers to your questions, know that God cares.

Jesus is your King. He gives justice and makes your paths straight. Stay close to Him. Use this new day to draw near to Him. He has judged you free and forgiven. Take that verdict and let your light shine for the people around you to see your beautiful Judge and Savior.

Dear Lord, I pray for Your justice to be served today. I see and hear things that are happening in our country and around the world that aren't fair. I pray that You would protect Your people and save the lost from their sins. Fix our broken world by Your powerful hands. Save us, God.

Help us all to wait on You, God. I pray that You would open the eyes of those people who are spiritually blind. I pray that they would see Your beautiful truth and know that Jesus is their personal King. As this happens, I pray that healing would come in the wake of these soul changes. Help me to have the courage to say I'm sorry.

I pray for the right words when
I speak to my friends about Your
giving heart. Use me to spread Your
goodness, Lord. Help me to do these
things so my life can be an example
that points others to Your justice.

BETRAYED

Do not fret when people succeed in their ways,
when they carry out their wicked schemes.
PSALM 37:7

. . . .

If you feel like someone betrayed you and your heart is heavy, find your peace in Jesus. This is what it looked like when He was betrayed, and it wasn't pretty:

Jesus had a very close friend by the name of Judas. Judas lived every day with Jesus, hearing Him teach and seeing Him do the work of God the Father. Jesus didn't have a lot of close friends, so you can imagine that Jesus and Judas and the other eleven disciples were a very tight group. But one day, Judas decided to betray Jesus in exchange for money.

The Bible says that when Jesus was praying in the garden, Judas walked up to Him and greeted Him with a kiss. This was the signal for the guards, who then quickly arrested Jesus (Matthew 26).

If you've been hurt by a friend, go to Jesus, and let Him hold you. He will understand your bad feelings and fill your heart with His true love.

Lord, I want to lift my voice to You and let this prayer be one of thanks for every good thing You've given me. You're showing me what it means to follow You. I realize that even though I'm dealing with the feelings of being betrayed, I do not want to betray You.

God, please forgive me every time I start to take Your love for granted. Help me remember how Jesus was betrayed. Help me remember that He allowed Himself to be handed over and crucified, all so that I may live. I can't comprehend that kind of love, but I'm so grateful for every bit of it.

God, I pray from a thankful heart
for Your will to be done. I'm so
grateful to know that You will never
betray me or let me go. I pray
my life will always tell the world
of Your great name!

Not Smart Enough

Not that we are competent in ourselves
to claim anything for ourselves,
but our competence comes from God.
2 Corinthians 3:5

• •

Think about everything that Jesus did for you. If you start to doubt your worth, consider Him today. If you find yourself not feeling smart enough at school or at home, remember that everything in your life comes from Him. He is your strength and your wisdom. Jesus is your power and your ability to make smart decisions.

Don't spend time comparing yourself to others. You are perfect just the way you are, because you are exactly how God made you. Instead, spend your days praying and asking God to show you all the ways He made you wonderful and how you can serve Him with those gifts.

No matter how weak or helpless you may feel, God is always holding you up. He is always keeping your feet from stumbling. He is your forever shield. Keep trusting in Him because He is worthy. He will never stop helping you. He will never stop protecting you. He will never stop loving you.

Dear God, I can't stop comparing myself to my friends. I know this is not the way You want me to live my life, so I'm asking you to forgive me. I don't feel smart. My grades are average, but I feel like I can do better. Please help me to do my best in school.

☆ ☆ ☆

I'm sorry for the times I don't feel like I'm smart enough. Please keep lifting me up when I fall short of understanding that You are proud of me.

Help me believe Your promises, Lord. Help me see each task that I'm given as an opportunity to rely on You more. Help me rely on Your wisdom and knowledge. Thank You for being with me and making me smart in Your eyes. Jesus, I want to have confidence in myself. I want to be proud of the skills You gave me and use them to help other people.

About the Author

Matt Koceich is a husband, father, and public school teacher. Matt and his family live in Texas.